EXPLORE OUTER SPACE

MARS

by Ruth Owen

WINDMILL BOOKS

New York

Published in 2014 by Windmill Books, An Imprint of Rosen Publishing
29 East 21st Street, New York, NY 10010

Produced for Windmill by Ruby Tuesday Books Ltd
Editor for Ruby Tuesday Books Ltd: Mark J. Sachner
US Editor: Sara Howell
Designer: Emma Randall
Consultant: Kevin Yates, Fellow of the Royal Astronomical Society

Photo Credits:
Cover, © Shutterstock; 1, 4–5, 5 (top), 6–7, 8–9, 10–11, 12–13, 14–15, 16–17, 19, 20–21, 22–23,
24–25, 26–27, 28–29 © NASA.

Library of Congress Cataloging-in-Publication Data

Owen, Ruth, 1967–
 Mars / by Ruth Owen.
    p. cm. — (Explore outer space)
 Includes index.
 ISBN 978-1-61533-725-5 (library binding) — ISBN 978-1-61533-767-5 (pbk.) —
 ISBN 978-1-61533-768-2 (6-pack)
 1. Mars (Planet)—Juvenile literature. 2. Mars (Planet)—Exploration—Juvenile literature. I.
Title. II. Series: Owen, Ruth, 1967– Explore outer space.
 QB641.O93 2014
 523.43—dc23
                                             2013005455

Manufactured in the United States of America

CPSIA Compliance Information: Batch # BS13WM: For Further Information contact Windmill Books, New York, New York at 1-866-478-0556

CONTENTS

THE RED PLANET

When the ancient Romans looked to the night sky, they saw a light that glowed red. They named this reddish-orange, or blood-colored, light Mars, after their god of war.

The Romans only knew what they could see with their eyes. Today, however, telescopes on Earth, spacecraft **orbiting** Mars, and even **rovers** that have landed on Mars, have uncovered many of the secrets of the **planet**. Today, we know Mars looks red because the soil on its surface is coated in iron oxide, or rust. We also know that our neighbor in the **solar system** is much smaller than Earth. It has a diameter of just 4,212 miles (6,779 km), compared to Earth's diameter of 7,918 miles (12,742 km).

Scientists have discovered that the fourth planet from the Sun is home to deserts, giant volcanoes, and vast areas covered with ice. We know more than our sky-gazing ancestors could ever have imagined. However, Mars, or "The Red Planet" as it is sometimes called, still has many intriguing mysteries to be solved!

That's Out of This World!

Mars' circumference at its equator is 13,233 miles (21,297 km) around. If you drove a car at 60 miles per hour (97 km/h) without stopping, a nonstop road trip around Mars would take just over nine days.

This image of Mars was taken in 2003 by the Hubble Space Telescope, which is in orbit around Earth.

The Sun

This incredible image shows a view of the Sun setting from the surface of Mars. It was captured in 2006 by **NASA**'s robot rover, *Spirit*, which was exploring the surface of Mars.

THE BIRTH OF A SOLAR SYSTEM

Mars, Earth, and the other planets in the solar system were created when our Sun formed about 4.5 billion years ago.

Before our solar system formed, there was a huge cloud of gas and dust in space. Over time, the cloud collapsed on itself, forming a massive spinning sphere, or ball. Around the sphere, a disk formed from the remaining gas and dust. The sphere pulled in more gas and dust, adding to its size, weight, and **gravity**. Pressure built up in the core, or center, of the sphere, causing the core to get hotter and hotter. Finally, the temperature inside the sphere became so hot that it ignited. A new **star**, our Sun, was born!

Inside the disk of rotating gas and dust around the Sun, other masses formed. These masses became the solar system's eight planets. Mercury is the closest planet to the Sun. Next comes Venus, then Earth, Mars, Jupiter, Saturn, Uranus, and finally Neptune.

Sun

Venus

Mars

Mercury

Earth

Jupiter

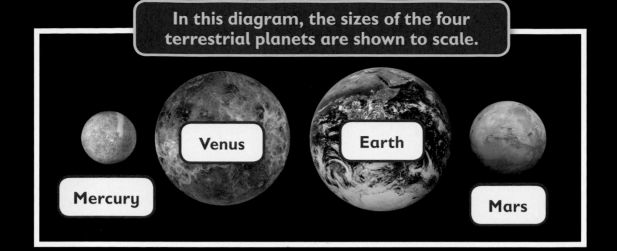

In this diagram, the sizes of the four terrestrial planets are shown to scale.

Mercury

Venus

Earth

Mars

That's Out of This World!

Mercury, Venus, Earth, and Mars are solid, rocky planets. They are known as the terrestrial planets. The word terrestrial comes from the Latin word *terra*, which means "earth" or "land."

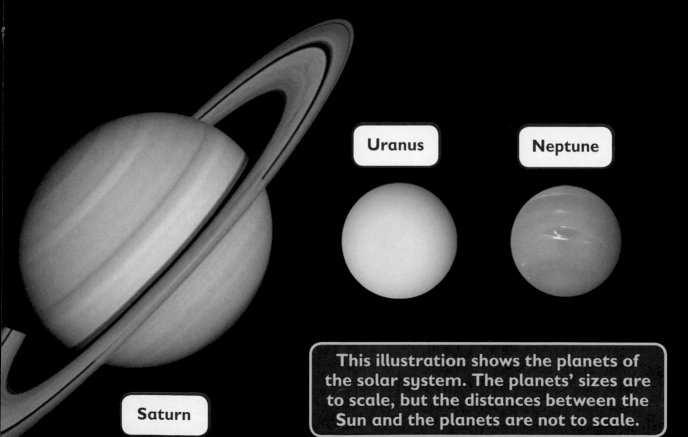

Uranus

Neptune

Saturn

This illustration shows the planets of the solar system. The planets' sizes are to scale, but the distances between the Sun and the planets are not to scale.

YEARS AND DAYS ON MARS

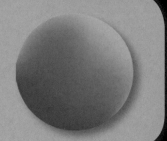

Like all the planets in the solar system, Mars is orbiting the Sun.

The length of time that a planet takes to orbit the Sun is known as a year. For example, a year on Earth lasts for 365 days. Mars is much further from the Sun than Earth, so it takes 687 days to travel around the Sun once. This means a year on Mars is nearly twice as long as a year on Earth.

Like Earth, Mars is slightly tilted on its **axis**, and this causes Mars to have seasons as we do on Earth. As Mars orbits the Sun, for some of the time the top half, or northern hemisphere, of the planet is tilted toward the Sun. This causes temperatures in the northern hemisphere to rise, so it is summer. Then the southern hemisphere, or bottom half, takes its turn to have summer, while the northern hemisphere is tilted away from the Sun and experiences winter.

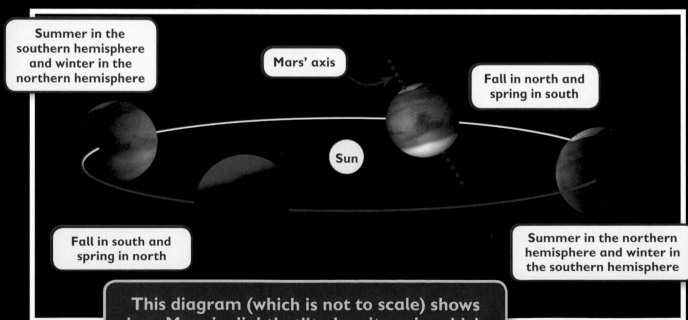

Summer in the southern hemisphere and winter in the northern hemisphere

Mars' axis

Fall in north and spring in south

Sun

Fall in south and spring in north

Summer in the northern hemisphere and winter in the southern hemisphere

This diagram (which is not to scale) shows how Mars is slightly tilted on its axis, which causes the planet to experience seasons.

To make one full orbit of the Sun, Mars travels nearly 889 million miles (1.4 billion km). It travels through space at an average speed of 53,858 miles per hour (86,677 km/h).

That's Out of This World!

As a planet orbits the Sun, it is also rotating, or spinning, on its axis. Earth takes just under 24 hours, a time period we call a day, to make one full rotation. Mars rotates at nearly the same speed as Earth, so a day on Mars is the same length as a day on Earth.

PHOBOS AND DEIMOS

Mars is not alone as it travels through space. It has two small traveling companions. These are its moons, Phobos and Deimos, which are orbiting the planet.

Phobos and Deimos look like rocky, lumpy potatoes. No one knows for sure how the moons came to be in orbit around Mars. It is likely they are **asteroids** that came too close to Mars and were captured by its gravity.

Phobos orbits Mars just 3,700 miles (6,000 km) above the planet's surface. It is so close to Mars, it can orbit the planet three times in every 24-hour period. Deimos is further away and takes about 30 hours to make one orbit.

The spacecraft *Mars Express*, which is orbiting Mars and studying the planet, has found evidence that suggests Phobos may not be a single solid rock. It could actually be a collection of smaller rocks and rubble tightly held together by gravity to form a single body.

Deimos, the smaller of Mars' two moons, is about 9 miles (15 km) across at its widest point.

Phobos, the larger of Mars' two moons, is about 17 miles (27 km) across at its widest point. It has a large crater, named the Stickney Crater, on one side.

Stickney Crater

That's Out of This World!

Mars' two moons were discovered in 1877 by an American astronomer named Asaph Hall. He named the moons Phobos and Deimos after the twin sons of Ares, the Greek god of war."Phobos" means "fear" and "panic," while "Deimos" means "flight," "dread," and "terror."

THE WEATHER TODAY IS DUSTY AND WINDY

Just like Earth, Mars is surrounded by an **atmosphere** made up of gases. Mars' atmosphere is about 100 times thinner than Earth's, though.

Mars' atmosphere is mostly made up of carbon dioxide with just a small amount of nitrogen and other gases. Unlike Earth's atmosphere, it contains only a trace of oxygen. If humans were ever to visit Mars, they would not be able to stand on the planet's surface and breathe unless they were wearing breathing equipment attached to tanks of oxygen.

The movement of gases in Mars' atmosphere causes winds to blow over the planet's surface, just as movements of air cause wind on Earth. The winds on Mars whip up the dust that covers the planet's surface. These winds often create massive dust storms that can cover the whole planet for weeks.

That's Out of This World!

Mars is much farther than Earth from the Sun. So while temperatures do go up and down with the seasons and from day to night, the average temperature on Mars is -67°F (-55°C).

The sky on Mars looks pinkish-orange because of red dust particles in the atmosphere.

Atmosphere

Surface of Mars

Dust devil

This image shows a dust devil (viewed from above) traveling across the surface of Mars. The whirlwind of dust was about .5 mile (800 m) high.

MARS, INSIDE AND OUT

The dusty, rocky surface of Mars is a fascinating world of huge impact craters, canyons, and volcanoes.

Beneath the surface, Mars is very similar to Earth. At its center is a solid core of metal made up mostly of iron. The core is surrounded by a layer called the mantle. This layer is made up of **molten** rock and metal. The outer crust of the planet is formed from a thick layer of rock.

The surface of Mars is scarred by many impact craters. These are created when asteroids and **meteoroids** smash into the planet's surface.

Mars is also home to the largest canyon in the solar system, Valles Marineris. The canyon is over eight times the length of the Grand Canyon and in places is over three times as deep! The massive canyon runs along Mars' equator. It probably formed when the planet's outer crust moved and cracked billions of years ago when Mars was still a young planet.

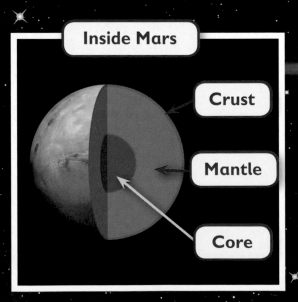

Inside Mars

Crust

Mantle

Core

That's Out of This World!

Mars has less mass than Earth, so the gravity on its surface is only about 38 percent of the surface gravity on Earth. This means if you weigh 100 pounds (45 kg) on Earth, you would weigh only 38 pounds (17 kg) on Mars.

This image shows huge dunes (artificially colored blue by computer) on Mars. The dunes form when dust is blown by the wind and collects in vast mounds.

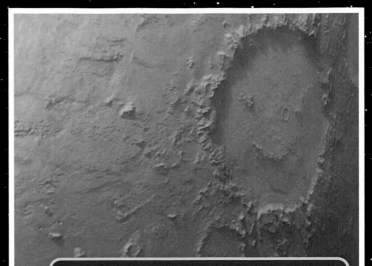

This impact crater on Mars is named the Galle Crater, or "Happy Face Crater." It is about 134 miles (215 km) wide.

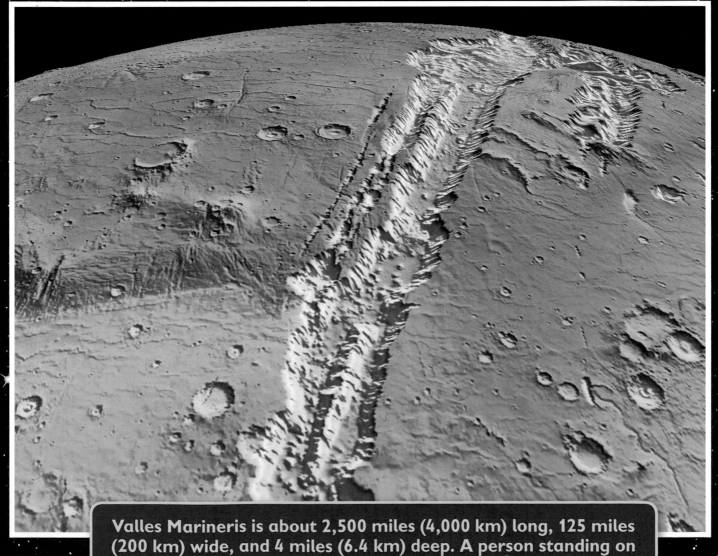

Valles Marineris is about 2,500 miles (4,000 km) long, 125 miles (200 km) wide, and 4 miles (6.4 km) deep. A person standing on one side would not be able to see the other side!

A MONSTER VOLCANO

Mars is not only home to the solar system's largest canyon. It also boasts the largest mountain on any planet in the solar system.

Olympus Mons is a massive volcano that is 16 miles (24 km) high from its base to its highest point. That's three times the height of Mount Everest, the tallest mountain on Earth.

Olympus Mons is no longer active, or erupting. In its past, however, eruption after eruption poured **lava** from its crater, which then hardened and over time formed the mountain's sloping sides. The volcano is so massive that at its base, the slopes have collapsed under their own weight to form steep cliffs that are nearly 2 miles (3 km) high.

It's hard to imagine the vast size of this monster volcano. If Olympus Mons were set down on Earth, though, it would cover an area the size of Arizona!

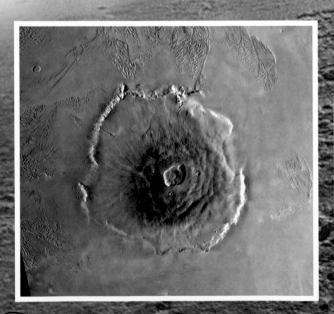

This view of Olympus Mons from above was created from images captured by *Viking 1*, a spacecraft that visited Mars in the late 1970s.

That's Out of This World!

Olympus Mons is a shield volcano. This type of volcano has gently sloping sides made from many layers of lava that have cooled and hardened to form a type of rock called basalt. Shield volcanoes get their name because their gently curved, circular shape looks like a warrior's shield.

Mars' atmosphere

Slopes of Olympus Mons

Steep cliffs

This 3-D illustration of Olympus Mons was created on a computer using measurements collected by equipment aboard the *Mars Global Surveyor* spacecraft.

MYSTERIOUS MARS

Since ancient times, people have been watching Mars in the night sky. Over the centuries, some people began to wonder if our neighboring planet might be home to an alien civilization.

In the late 1800s, an Italian astronomer named Giovanni Schiaparelli studied Mars through a telescope. Schiaparelli said he could see strange lines on the planet that he called *canali*, which is the Italian word for "channels." Some people translated *canali* to mean "canals," which are artificial rivers constructed by people. The lines seemed to join at dark, greenish areas on the planet's surface. An American astronomer, Percival Lowell, became excited about the idea that the lines could be canals built by Martians to carry water from wet areas to dry places where plants were being grown.

When spacecraft visited Mars in the 1960s, however, they sent back images of a dry landscape. The lines, or canals, were just a trick of the light when people looked through telescopes. There were no canals, no plants, and no aliens!

That's Out of This World!

In 1976, the *Viking 1* spacecraft took a photograph of Mars that seemed to show a giant rocky face. Some people suggested the face had been carved by an alien civilization. Today, many spacecraft have visited and photographed Mars, and we know the face was simply caused by light and shadow on a massive rocky Martian hill!

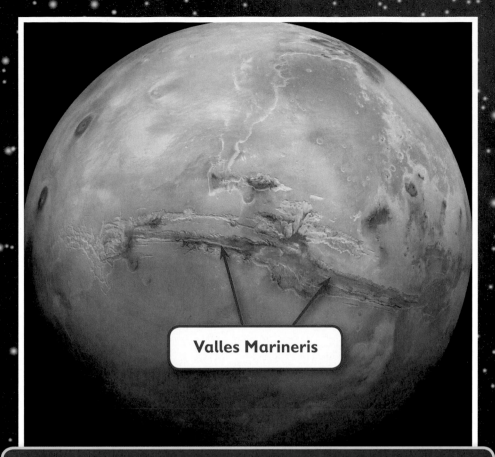

Valles Marineris

Images sent back to Earth by spacecraft have not shown any aliens, but they have shown incredible landscape features such as Valles Marineris.

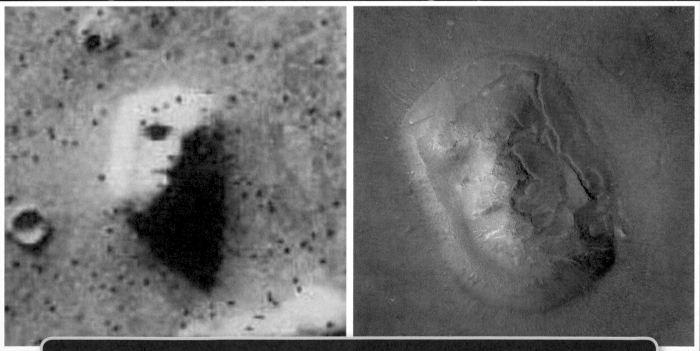

The image of "the face on Mars" (left) was taken by *Viking 1* in 1976. Just over 20 years later, the *Mars Reconnaissance Orbiter* took a high-resolution image (right) of the same rocky hill.

Is There Water on Mars?

When spacecraft began to visit Mars in the 1960s, they found no canals, rivers, oceans, or liquid water. There is, however, lots of ice and evidence there was once liquid water on Mars.

Just like Earth, Mars has large areas of ice, called ice caps, at its north and south poles. The top layer of the ice caps is made up of dry ice, which is frozen carbon dioxide gas. Below the dry ice, however, there is frozen water. There is also lots of frozen water underground, just as there is frozen water in the ground in **Arctic** regions on Earth.

Billions of years ago, however, it was a different story. Valleys carved across the land and marks in rocks show that liquid water once flowed over the planet's surface. Today, Mars is too cold for liquid water to exist. So what caused Mars' **climate** to change? When did the water disappear? And was Mars once a water-covered, warm planet like Earth?

The polar ice cap at Mars' north pole measures about 600 miles (1,000 km) across.

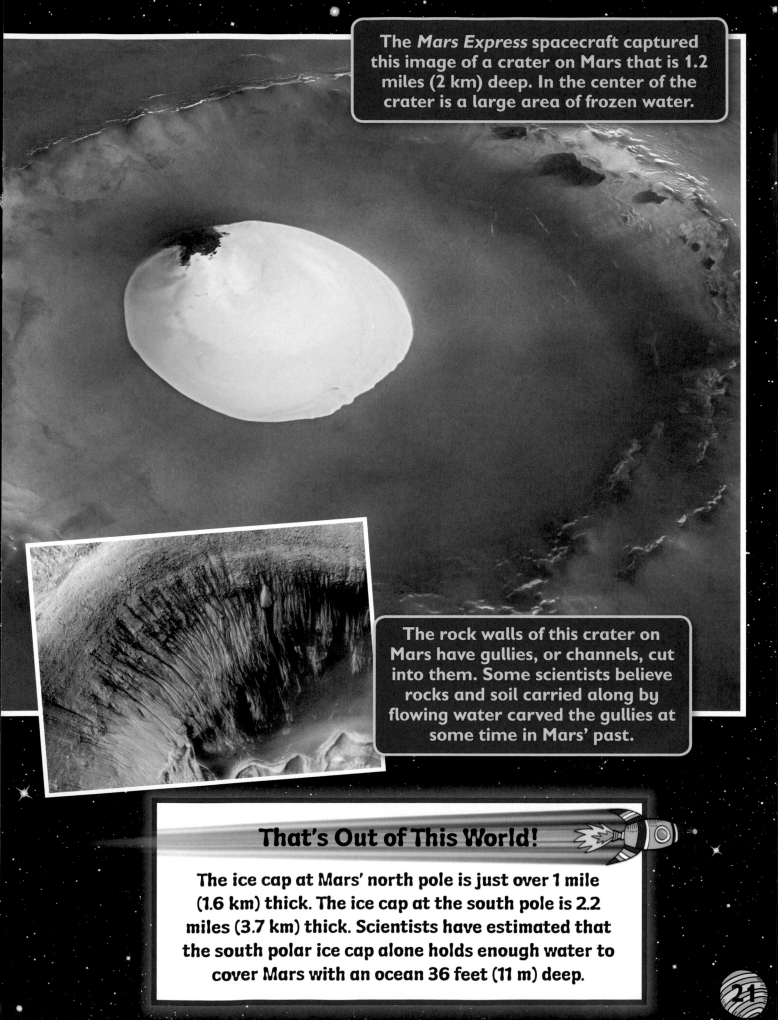

The *Mars Express* spacecraft captured this image of a crater on Mars that is 1.2 miles (2 km) deep. In the center of the crater is a large area of frozen water.

The rock walls of this crater on Mars have gullies, or channels, cut into them. Some scientists believe rocks and soil carried along by flowing water carved the gullies at some time in Mars' past.

That's Out of This World!

The ice cap at Mars' north pole is just over 1 mile (1.6 km) thick. The ice cap at the south pole is 2.2 miles (3.7 km) thick. Scientists have estimated that the south polar ice cap alone holds enough water to cover Mars with an ocean 36 feet (11 m) deep.

EXPLORING MARS

Many spacecraft have been sent to Mars to study the planet. Some have orbited Mars, studying it from space, while others have landed on its surface.

When the orbits of Earth and Mars bring the two planets close together, it can take as little as six months for a spacecraft to reach Mars.

In 1976, the *Viking 1* and *Viking 2* landers were the first spacecraft to land on Mars. The landers photographed the planet's surface and studied its atmosphere and soil.

At the start of 2013, there were three spacecraft orbiting Mars. NASA's *2001 Mars Odyssey* has been studying Mars since 2001. One of its tasks is to transmit messages from rovers on the surface of Mars back to Earth.

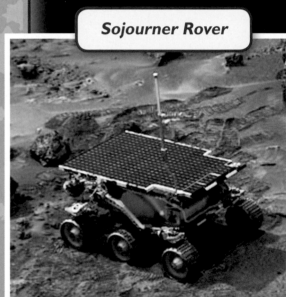

Sojourner Rover

The European Space Agency's *Mars Express* spacecraft has been in orbit since 2003. Part of its mission is to study the history of liquid water on the planet. NASA's *Mars Reconnaissance Orbiter* is looking for evidence of ancient Martian seas and studying changes in Mars' climate.

That's Out of This World!

The first rover, or moving robot, to land on Mars was the *Sojourner Rover* in July 1997. The six-wheeled vehicle was just 2 feet (65 cm) long and 1 foot (30 cm) tall. *Sojourner* traveled over the surface of Mars, examining rocks and soil for 83 days before it was shut down.

2001 Mars Odyssey

Mars Express

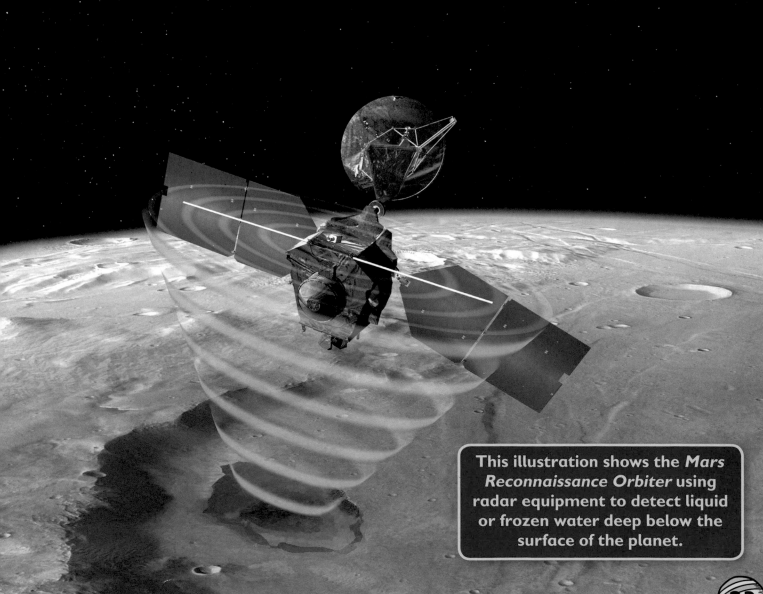

This illustration shows the *Mars Reconnaissance Orbiter* using radar equipment to detect liquid or frozen water deep below the surface of the planet.

ROBOT GEOLOGISTS

In January 2004, NASA's twin rovers *Spirit* and *Opportunity* landed on Mars on opposite sides of the planet. The mission of the two robotic **geologists** was to study Mars' rocks and soil for clues to its watery past.

A human geologist walks from place to place examining rocks with handheld tools. The robotic rovers were controlled by human operators on Earth and could drive up to 130 feet (40 m) in a day. Each rover was fitted with a robotic arm and many different scientific instruments for studying rocks and carrying out experiments.

During their mission, the rovers have discovered plenty of evidence in Mars' rocks and soil to show that Mars was once a planet with liquid water.

Spirit worked for over six years until it became stuck in sand and NASA had to terminate its mission. At the start of 2013, *Opportunity* was still exploring the surface of Mars. The robot geologist, which was originally designed to work for just three months, was still going strong!

That's Out of This World!

The robotic arms of *Spirit* and *Opportunity* contained cameras that could zoom in on a rock and take highly detailed photos. Back on Earth, a human scientist could analyze the photo in the same way as if he or she had been able to hold a magnifying glass to the actual rock.

This illustration shows one of the twin rovers at work on the surface of Mars.

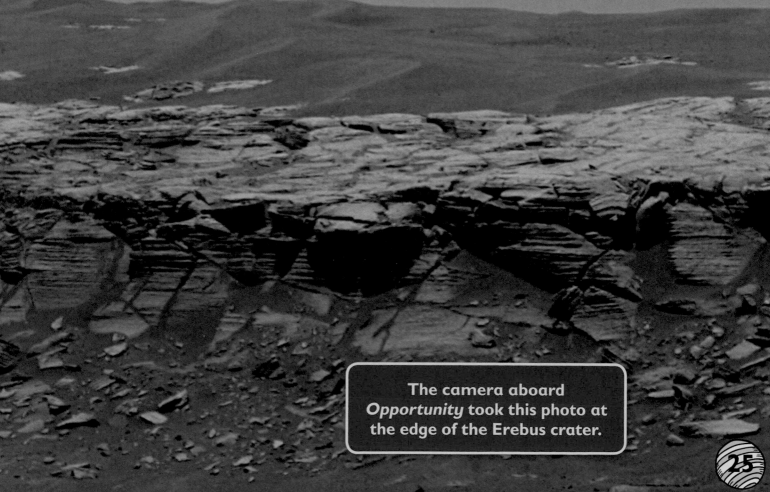

The camera aboard *Opportunity* took this photo at the edge of the Erebus crater.

A Robot Laboratory

In August 2012, a robot rover named *Curiosity* landed on the surface of Mars. *Curiosity* is part of NASA's Mars Science Laboratory Mission.

Curiosity is about the size of an SUV. It is a huge vehicle compared to tiny *Sojourner*, the first robot to travel on the surface of Mars, which was about the size of a microwave oven!

Safely encased inside a spacecraft, *Curiosity* blasted out of Earth's atmosphere aboard an Atlas V rocket in November 2011. The spacecraft traveled the millions of miles (km) to Mars and entered the planet's atmosphere. The spacecraft then descended on a parachute. In the final seconds, the descent stage craft and *Curiosity* emerged from the spacecraft. The descent stage then acted like a crane and lowered *Curiosity* to the ground on tethers.

Curiosity's adventure begins aboard a rocket on November 26, 2011, at Cape Canaveral Air Force Station, Florida.

That's Out of This World!

Previous rovers, and the landing craft carrying them, fell to the surface of Mars encased in airbags to cushion their fall. *Curiosity* was too large and heavy to land in this way without being damaged.

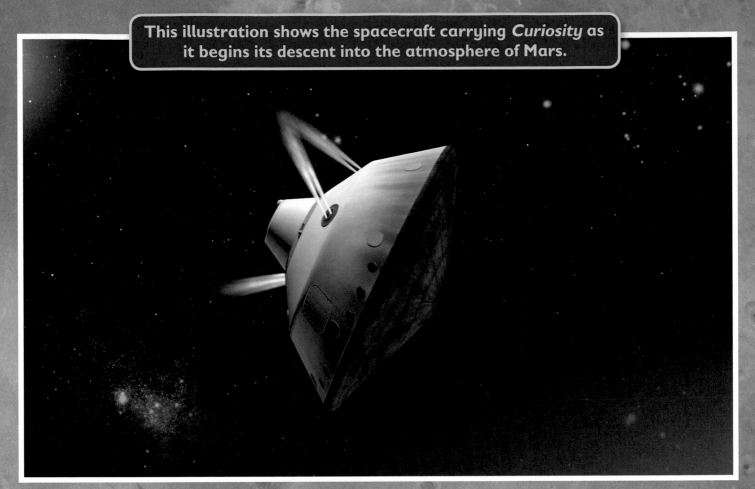

This illustration shows the spacecraft carrying *Curiosity* as it begins its descent into the atmosphere of Mars.

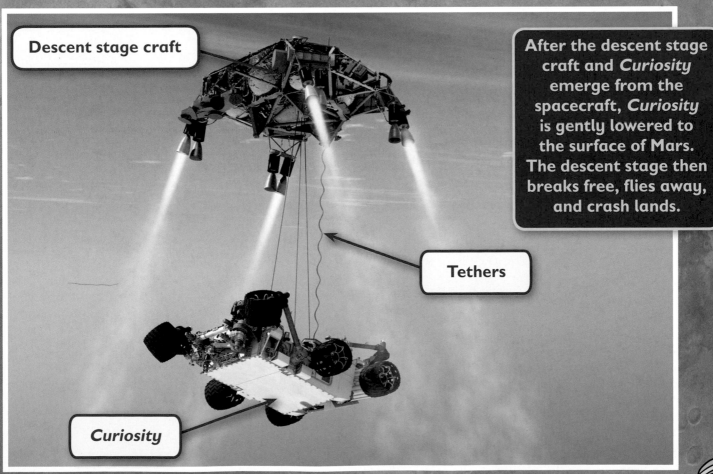

Descent stage craft

After the descent stage craft and *Curiosity* emerge from the spacecraft, *Curiosity* is gently lowered to the surface of Mars. The descent stage then breaks free, flies away, and crash lands.

Tethers

Curiosity

Uncovering Mars' Secrets

Water is essential for living things to survive. If Mars was once a warmer planet and had liquid water, perhaps it was home to living things!

The *Curiosity* rover will analyze soil and rocks on Mars. It will look for chemical clues that Mars could once have been a suitable place for life to exist. If there was life on Mars, it would not have been intelligent alien beings, but **microscopic** life-forms called **microbes**.

In 1984, scientists found a small **meteorite** that had crashed into Earth from Mars. Inside the rock, they found microscopic tubelike shapes. Some scientists believed the shapes could be the **fossils** of microbes that lived on Mars billions of years ago. Other scientists did not agree with this idea.

The first living things on Earth were microscopic microbes. Was Mars once home to microbes, too? Millions of miles (km) from Earth, *Curiosity* is searching for clues to help solve the mystery. Will it find signs of microscopic life? Will it find something amazing that we've not yet imagined? Only time and science will tell!

ALH84001,0

That's Out of This World!

Curiosity is able to roll over obstacles up to 30 inches (75 cm) high and is able to travel at about 100 feet (30 meters) per hour. The rover can use a camera on its robotic arm to take photos of itself to send back to Earth. These photos enable *Curiosity*'s human operators to check how the robot is holding up during its mission.

This is a self-portrait taken by the *Curiosity* robot using a camera on its robotic arm. You might expect to see the arm disappearing out of view, but the image was pieced together using 55 different shots with the arm in a different position each time. Therefore, the arm does not appear.

GLOSSARY

Arctic (ARK-tik) The northernmost area on Earth, which includes northern parts of Europe, Asia, and North America, the Arctic Ocean, the polar ice cap, and the North Pole.

asteroids (AS-teh-roydz) Rocky objects orbiting the Sun and ranging in size from a few feet (m) to hundreds of miles (km) in diameter.

astronomer (uh-STRAH-nuh-mer) A scientist who specializes in the study of outer space.

atmosphere (AT-muh-sfeer) The layer of gases surrounding a planet, moon, or star.

axis (AK-sus) An imaginary line about which a body, such as a planet, rotates.

climate (KLY-mut) The average temperature and weather conditions in a particular place over a long period of time.

equator (ih-KWAY-tur) An imaginary line drawn around a planet that is an equal distance from the north and south poles.

fossils (FO-sulz) Imprints of the remains of an animal, plant, or other living thing that has formed in rocks over millions of years.

geologists (jee-AH-luh-jists) Scientists who studies rocks and soil.

gravity (GRA-vuh-tee) The force that causes objects to be attracted toward Earth's center or toward other physical bodies in space, such as stars, planets, and moons.

laboratory (LA-bruh-tor-ee) A room, building, and sometimes a vehicle, where there is equipment that can be used to carry out experiments and other scientific studies.

lava (LAH-vuh) Rock that has been heated within a planet, moon, or asteroid to the point where it flows like a liquid.

meteorite (MEE-tee-uh-ryt) A piece of an asteroid that has survived the fall to the surface of a planet or moon.

meteoroids (MEE-tee-uh-roydz) Small particles or fragments that have broken free from an asteroid.

microbes (MY-krohbz) Tiny living things, such as bacteria, which can only be seen with a microscope.

microscopic (my-kreh-SKAH-pik) Only visible through a microscope, not with the naked eye.

molten (MOHL-ten) Melted, or liquefied, by heat.

orbiting (OR-bih-ting) Circling in a curved path around another object.

planet (PLA-net) An object in space that is of a certain size and that orbits, or circles, a star.

rover (ROH-vur) A robotic wheeled vehicle used to explore a planet.

solar system (SOH-ler SIS-tem) The Sun and everything that orbits around it, including planets and their moons, asteroids, meteoroids, and comets.

star (STAR) A body in space that produces its own heat and light through the release of nuclear energy created within its core.

WEBSITES

For web resources related to the subject of this book, go to: www.windmillbooks.com/weblinks and select this book's title.

READ MORE

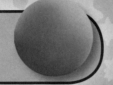

Landau, Elaine. *Mars*. A True Book. Danbury, CT: Children's Press, 2008.

Rusch, Elizabeth. *The Mighty Mars Rover: The Incredible Adventures of Spirit and Opportunity*. Scientists in the Field. New York: Houghton Mifflin Books for Children, 2013.

Simon, Seymour. *Destination: Mars*. New York: HarperCollins, 2004.

INDEX